Grandmother's Words of Wisdom

A KEEPSAKE JOURNAL OF STORIES, LIFE LESSONS, AND FAMILY MEMORIES FOR MY GRANDCHILD

Grandmother's Words of Wisdom

A KEEPSAKE JOURNAL OF STORIES, LIFE LESSONS, AND FAMILY MEMORIES FOR MY GRANDCHILD

Laura Buller

Bluestreak
BOOKS

Bluestreak

an imprint of Weldon Owen International
PO Box 3088
San Rafael, CA 94912
www.weldonowen.com

© 2021 Weldon Owen

Library of Congress Cataloging in Publication data is available.

Printed in China

ISBN-13: 978-1-68188-628-2

10 9 8 7 6 5 4 3 2 1

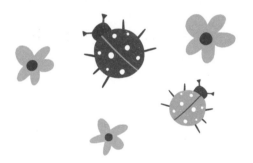

Contents

Introduction

A Private Note to Grandkids

Grandmothers certainly know a lot, but they might not always tell you everything. Wouldn't you like to know all the things your grandmother has learned, hear about the experiences that have given her so much wisdom, and maybe catch a whisper of some of her secrets? This journal is here to help your grandmother pass along a whole generation's worth of advice. The prompts inside will help guide her through her life and its lessons. When she shares her thoughts with you, it will spark plenty of fascinating conversations, and become a real keepsake for you and your family. Enjoy sharing this book of your grandmother's wisdom.

A LETTER TO MY GRANDCHILD(REN), FROM MY HEART TO YOURS

Written on _____

As I write this, I am in _____

_____

_____

_____

_____

_____

_____

_____

_____

_____

_____

_____

_____

_____

_____

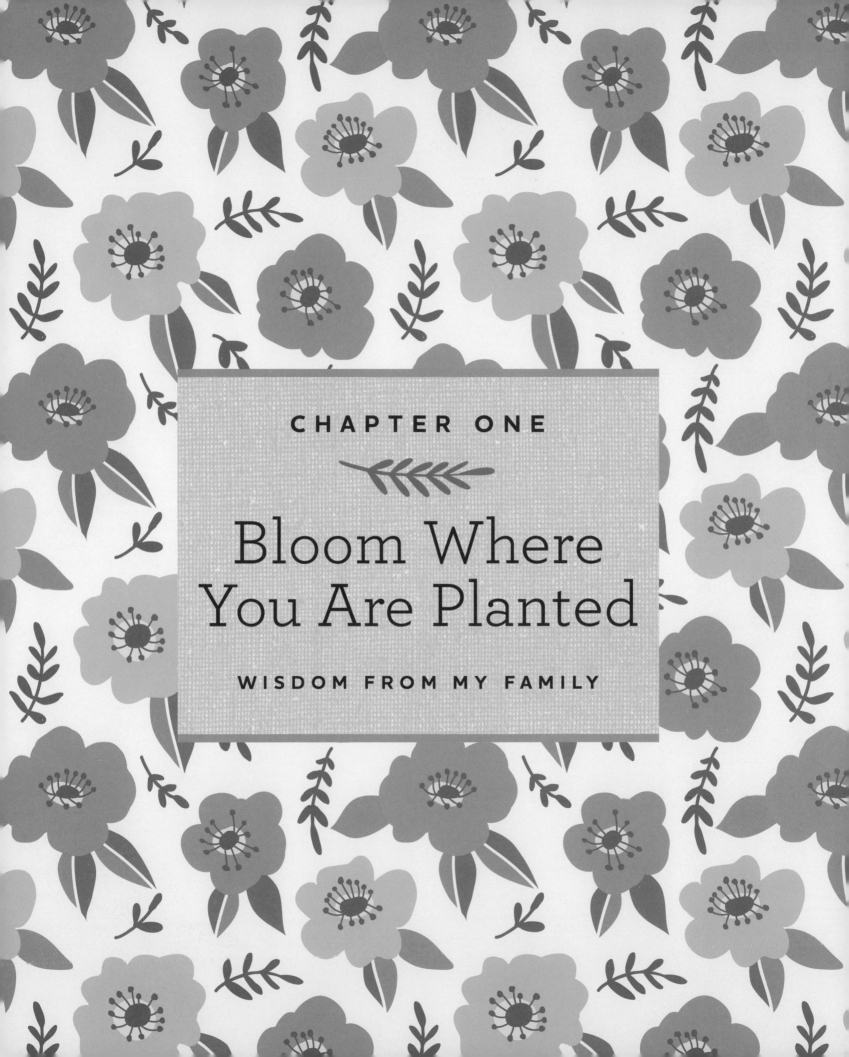

CHAPTER ONE

Bloom Where You Are Planted

WISDOM FROM MY FAMILY

About Me

A grandmother is a little bit parent, a little bit teacher, and a little bit best friend.

—UNKNOWN

I was born on _____

_____

I was born in _____

_____

A little bit about my family at the time _____

_____

_____

_____

_____

_____

_____

A special story I want to share about my family

_____

_____

_____

_____

_____

_____

_____

_____

_____

_____

_____

_____

_____

_____

_____

_____

_____

Our Family History

To forget one's ancestors is to be a brook without a source, a tree without a root.

—CHINESE PROVERB

Our family names are _____

_____

Our relatives came from _____

_____

_____

Some customs we observed from our heritage were _____

_____

_____

_____

_____

_____

We also shared these religious traditions _____

_____

_____

_____

_____

One life lesson I learned from my relatives is _____

_____

_____

_____

_____

A family saying I've heard all my life is _____

_____

_____

_____

_____

_____

Our family motto could be _____

_____

_____

_____

_____

_____

A Family Foundation

Call it a clan, call it a network, call it a tribe, call it a family: whatever you call it, whoever you are, you need one.

—JANE HOWARD

All in all, my early childhood was _____

_____

_____

_____

_____

I depended on my family for _____

_____

_____

_____

_____

_____

When I needed advice, the relative I turned to was _____

_____

_____

_____

The person who taught me the most was _____

_____

_____

_____

_____

Something my family passed down to me that I'd like you to know _____

_____

_____

_____

I am grateful to my family for teaching me _____

_____

_____

_____

_____

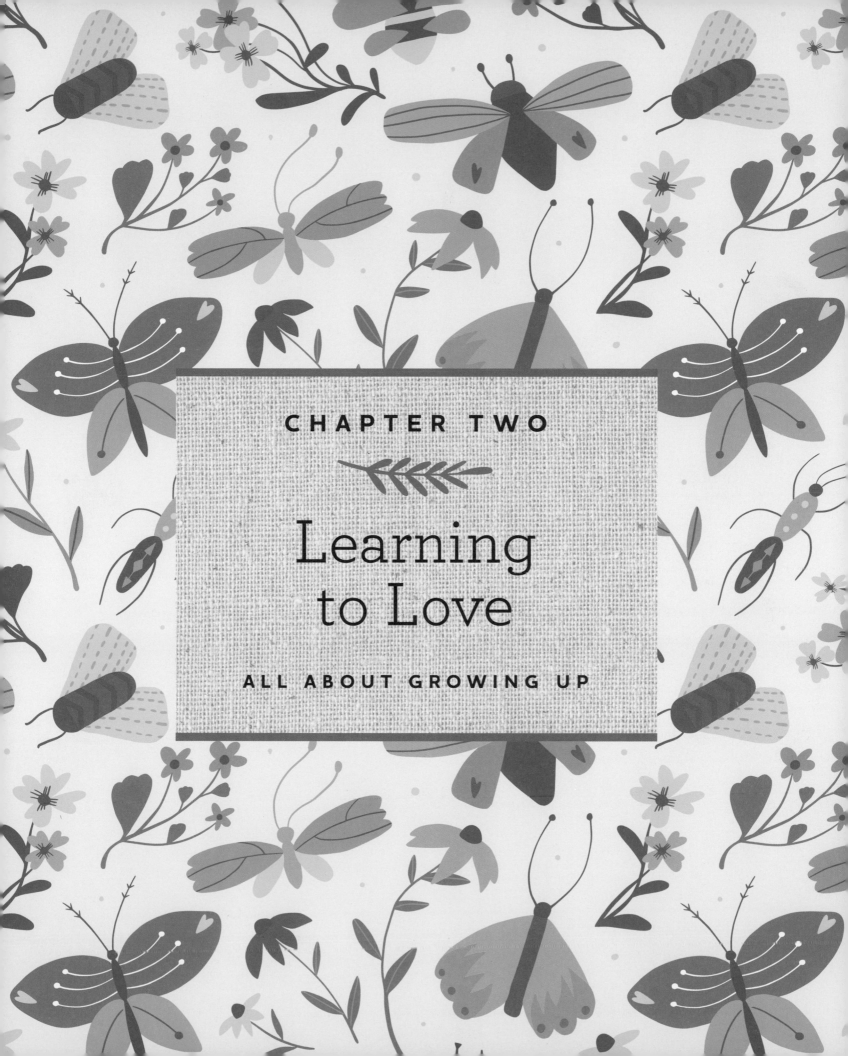

CHAPTER TWO

Learning to Love

ALL ABOUT GROWING UP

Learning and Growing

In school, you're taught a lesson and then given a test. In life, you're given a test that teaches you a lesson.

—TOM BODETT

For me, school was _____

_____

_____

_____

_____

_____

My favorite teacher was _____

_____

_____

_____

Some things I learned in class that I still remember are _____

_____

_____

_____

The important things I learned outside of the classroom were _____

_____

_____

_____

_____

I got through challenges at school by _____

_____

_____

_____

_____

My hopes and dreams for you at school are _____

_____

_____

_____

_____

Making Friends

Friends are the family
you choose.

—JESS C. SCOTT

Friendship is so important because _____

_____

_____

_____

_____

My best friends were _____

_____

_____

_____

_____

We loved to _____

_____

_____

_____

_____

A secret we shared together was _____

_____

_____

_____

_____

_____

My advice for making friends is _____

_____

_____

_____

_____

_____

Friendships can be tricky sometimes because _____

_____

_____

_____

_____

_____

A story about a time a friendship was tested _____

_____

_____

_____

_____

_____

_____

_____

_____

_____

_____

This is what I learned _____

_____

_____

_____

_____

_____

My advice for keeping good friends is _____

_____

_____

_____

_____

_____

I am grateful to my friends because _____

_____

_____

_____

_____

_____

My Family and Me

To us, family means putting your arms around each other and being there.

—BARBARA BUSH

As I grew older, my feelings about my family were _____

_____

_____

_____

I became close to _____

_____

_____

_____

_____

My family helped me to learn and grow by _____

_____

_____

_____

_____

One of my favorite memories from that time is _____

_____

_____

_____

_____

_____

_____

The best advice I had from my family was _____

_____

_____

_____

_____

_____

Becoming Me

Love yourself first and
everything falls into line.

—LUCILLE BALL

My teenage years weren't always easy, but I learned _____

_____

_____

_____

_____

I made mistakes sometimes, like _____

_____

_____

_____

_____

My advice to you is _____

_____

_____

_____

_____

_____

I learned to become more myself when _____

_____

_____

_____

_____

_____

One thing to always keep in mind is _____

_____

_____

_____

_____

_____

CHAPTER THREE

Moving On

LEAVING, LOVING, AND LEARNING

Leaving Home

Most things in my life I had before leaving home. Values, support, great family. I was shaped at an early age.

—SISSY SPACEK

I was ready to leave the nest when _____

_____

_____

_____

_____

How I felt about leaving home _____

_____

_____

_____

_____

_____

The things I looked forward to were _____

_____

_____

_____

_____

_____

I knew I would be sad about _____

_____

_____

_____

_____

_____

_____

_____

My advice to you when you are thinking of setting off on your own is _____

_____

_____

_____

_____

_____

_____

Independent Days

Where we love is home—
home that our feet may leave,
but not our hearts.

—OLIVER WENDELL HOLMES, SR.

A story about leaving home for the first time _____

_____

_____

_____

_____

The thing I missed the most was _____

_____

_____

_____

_____

_____

I was most proud of myself for _____

_____

_____

_____

_____

_____

A few mistakes I made were _____

_____

_____

_____

_____

_____

_____

The family advice that I remembered was _____

_____

_____

_____

_____

_____

_____

My brightest dreams for you when you leave home are _____

_____

_____

_____

_____

_____

_____

_____

_____

_____

_____

_____

_____

_____

_____

_____

_____

_____

My best advice to you for achieving those dreams is _____

_____

_____

_____

_____

_____

_____

_____

_____

_____

_____

_____

_____

_____

_____

_____

_____

How to Be an Adult

Growing up is hard, love.
Otherwise everyone
would do it.

—KIM HARRISON

I felt grown up for the first time when _____

_____

_____

_____

One thing I know now that I wish I'd known then is _____

_____

_____

_____

_____

I always want you to remember these things about standing on your own two feet

_____

_____

_____

_____

_____

_____

But it's always OK to _____

_____

_____

_____

_____

You know you're doing a great job when _____

_____

_____

_____

_____

_____

Love Is the Answer

First best is falling in love. Second best is being in love. Least best is falling out of love. But any of it is better than never having been in love.

—MAYA ANGELOU

Falling in love is so complicated because _____

_____

_____

One thing I'd like you to know about being in love is _____

_____

_____

_____

One thing I'd like you to know about heartbreak is _____

_____

_____

_____

I learned that you know you are in love when _____

_____

_____

_____

_____

A story about love in my own life that I want to share with you _____

_____

_____

_____

_____

_____

_____

_____

_____

_____

_____

_____

_____

Starting a Family

There is no such thing as a perfect parent. So just be a real one.

—SUE ATKINS

The story of how I decided to start a family is _____

_____

_____

_____

_____

_____

_____

_____

_____

I was excited because _____

_____

_____

_____

_____

_____

I was anxious about _____

_____

_____

_____

_____

_____

The things I wanted to pass down to my children were _____

_____

_____

_____

_____

_____

_____

Being a parent is a huge responsibility. I felt _____

_____

_____

_____

_____

_____

_____

When your parent was young _____

_____

_____

_____

_____

_____

_____

_____

I knew I was doing a good job when _____

_____

_____

_____

_____

_____

My advice if you decide to start a family of your own is _____

_____

_____

_____

_____

_____

_____

_____

_____

_____

_____

_____

_____

Family Love

A parent's love is whole
no matter how many
times divided.

—ROBERT BRAULT

Having children of my own taught me a lot about my own family. I learned

_____

_____

_____

_____

I was grateful to my family for _____

_____

_____

_____

_____

I wish I had known _____

_____

_____

_____

My family relationships changed because _____

_____

_____

_____

_____

A story about seeing my own children with my family members _____

_____

_____

_____

_____

_____

_____

_____

_____

CHAPTER FOUR

Home Truths

CREATING A
HAPPY HOME

A Happy Home

There is no place like home.

—L. FRANK BAUM

Let me tell you a little about our first family home _____

_____

_____

_____

_____

_____

_____

_____

_____

The thing I was proudest of was _____

_____

_____

_____

_____

What made it feel like home was _____

_____

_____

_____

_____

When my family visited I felt _____

_____

_____

_____

_____

I think you need these ingredients for a happy home _____

_____

_____

_____

_____

_____

Keepsakes and Memories

Is it good or bad that the defining items of life can fit into one small box?

—RUTA SEPTETYS

A keepsake I treasure is _____

_____

_____

_____

Another treasure that means the world to me is _____

_____

_____

_____

_____

Something you gave me that brings me happiness is _____

_____

And this is why _____

_____

_____

_____

_____

_____

What objects are worth holding on to _____

_____

_____

_____

_____

When it's okay to let go of something _____

_____

_____

_____

_____

My Wishes for Your Home

There's no place like home—except Grandma's.

—UNKNOWN

Little things can make your home a happy one. For example,

_____

_____

_____

_____

_____

_____

_____

_____

_____

You can bring happiness to your home and express your personality with

_____

_____

_____

_____

_____

_____

Some of my favorite spots in my own home are _____

_____

_____

_____

_____

_____

_____

_____

My advice for creating a comfortable home is _____

_____

_____

_____

_____

_____

From the Kitchen

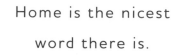

Home is the nicest
word there is.

—LAURA INGALLS WILDER

Food brings a family together. Here are my favorite recipes to share with family and friends.

_____

_____

Ingredients

_____   _____

_____   _____

_____   _____

_____   _____

_____   _____

Instructions _____

_____

_____

_____

_____

_____

_____

_____

_____

_____

_____

_____

_____

_____

_____

_____

_____

_____

Another delicious treat _____

_____

_____

Ingredients

_____   _____

_____   _____

_____   _____

_____   _____

_____   _____

_____   _____

_____   _____

Instructions _____

_____

_____

_____

_____

_____

_____

_____

One of our family's favorite holiday dishes _____

_____

_____

Ingredients

_____   _____

_____   _____

_____   _____

_____   _____

_____   _____

_____   _____

Instructions _____

_____

_____

_____

_____

_____

_____

_____

Another holiday recipe _____

_____

_____

Ingredients

_____   _____

_____   _____

_____   _____

_____   _____

_____   _____

_____   _____

Instructions _____

_____

_____

_____

_____

_____

_____

CHAPTER FIVE

Living a Great Life

FINDING JOY

Finding Happy

Happiness never decreases
by being shared.

—BUDDHA

The books that have made me smile are _____

_____

_____

_____

_____

Some of my favorite movies are _____

_____

_____

_____

_____

A painting I love is _____

_____

_____

The music that brings me happiness is _____

_____

_____

_____

_____

My favorite song of all is _____

_____

_____

My advice for finding art and music you love is _____

_____

_____

_____

_____

_____

_____

_____

_____

Something I love to do is _____

_____

_____

_____

_____

_____

I am never happier than when I am _____

_____

_____

_____

_____

_____

This is my perfect day _____

_____

_____

_____

_____

_____

I share my happy times with you when we _____

_____

_____

_____

_____

My advice for creating happy moments is _____

_____

_____

_____

_____

_____

_____

_____

_____

_____

_____

Making Love Bloom

Love is the flower you've got to let grow.

—JOHN LENNON

The love (or loves) of my life _____

_____

_____

_____

_____

_____

_____

_____

_____

If that love was a flower, it would be _____

_____

Because _____

_____

_____

_____

_____

_____

_____

_____

_____

I've learned this about love _____

_____

_____

_____

_____

_____

_____

_____

_____

_____

Do What You Love

If you do what you love, you'll never work a day in your life.

—MARC ANTHONY

The jobs I've held are _____

_____

_____

_____

_____

Every job is a learning experience, and I found out that _____

_____

_____

_____

_____

One job I will never forget was _____

_____

_____

_____

_____

My advice to you for choosing a career is _____

_____

_____

_____

_____

_____

_____

Always remember this about work _____

_____

_____

_____

_____

_____

_____

Staying Strong

Life is not waiting for the storms to pass. It's about learning to dance in the rain.

—VIVIAN GREENE

Life is full of ups and downs. But one thing is for sure _____

_____

_____

_____

I know this because _____

_____

_____

_____

_____

_____

_____

When life puts you to the test, remember _____

_____

_____

_____

_____

_____

_____

_____

In troubled times, picture me saying this to you _____

_____

_____

_____

_____

_____

_____

_____

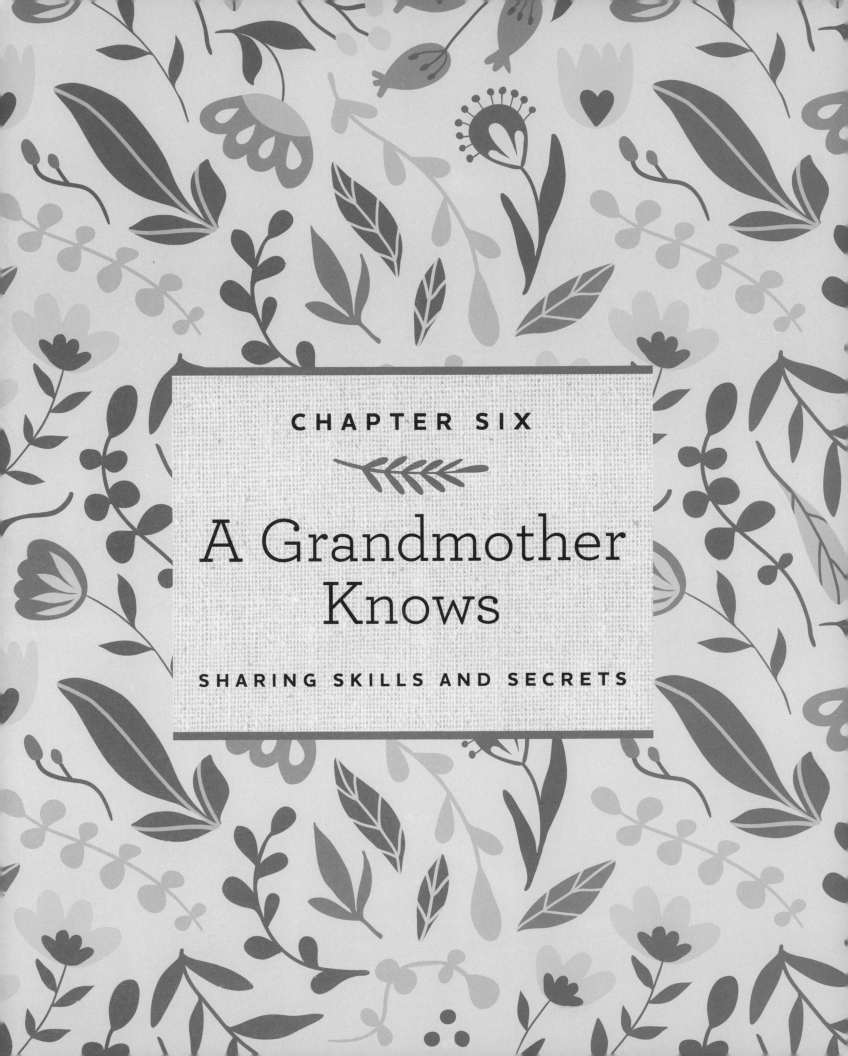

CHAPTER SIX

A Grandmother Knows

SHARING SKILLS AND SECRETS

Be Grateful

Feeling gratitude and not expressing it is like wrapping a present and not giving it.

—WILLIAM ARTHUR WARD

Take time to count your blessings, because _____

_____

_____

_____

_____

_____

Don't forget the little things like _____

_____

_____

_____

_____

One memorable time someone shared their thanks with me was

_____

_____

_____

_____

I'm grateful to you because _____

_____

_____

_____

This is the way I show it _____

_____

_____

_____

_____

When I look back on my life so far, I feel gratitude for _____

_____

_____

_____

_____

_____

Be Curious

The mind that opens to a new idea never returns to its original size.

—ALBERT EINSTEIN

It's important to stay curious throughout your life because _____

_____

_____

_____

_____

_____

Someone who nurtured my curiosity was _____

_____

_____

_____

When you were little, you were always curious about

_____

_____

_____

_____

_____

Here's something I'm curious about _____

_____

_____

_____

_____

_____

_____

_____

I find the best way to get answers is _____

_____

_____

_____

_____

_____

_____

Be Loving

Seize the moments of happiness, love and be loved! That is the only reality in the world. All else is folly.

—LEO TOLSTOY

Love is all you need because _____

_____

_____

_____

_____

Sometimes love isn't easy. For example, _____

_____

_____

_____

_____

This is why being a loving person is so important _____

_____

_____

_____

_____

_____

_____

These are the ways I've watched you show your love _____

_____

_____

_____

_____

_____

_____

Some ways I like to show my love are _____

_____

_____

_____

_____

_____

Be Positive

Be the reason someone smiles.
Be the reason someone feels
loved and believes in the
goodness of people.

—ROY T. BENNETT

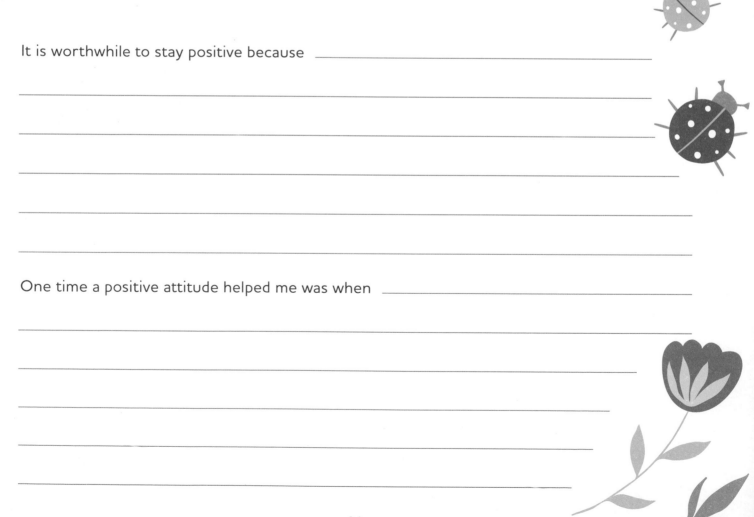

It is worthwhile to stay positive because _____

_____

_____

_____

_____

One time a positive attitude helped me was when _____

_____

_____

_____

_____

When I feel down, this is what I think to myself to feel better

_____

_____

_____

_____

_____

_____

This story always makes me laugh _____

_____

_____

_____

_____

_____

If life gives you lemons, you can make lemonade, or _____

_____

_____

_____

_____

_____

Be Yourself

Don't you ever let a soul in the world tell you that you can't be exactly who you are.

—LADY GAGA

Being true to yourself is so important because _____

_____

_____

_____

When I had my doubts about being myself, I thought _____

_____

_____

_____

_____

I learned to believe in myself by _____

_____

_____

_____

_____

Something unique about me that I may have passed down to you is _____

_____

_____

_____

_____

_____

_____

Some ways you can make the most of yourself are _____

_____

_____

_____

_____

_____

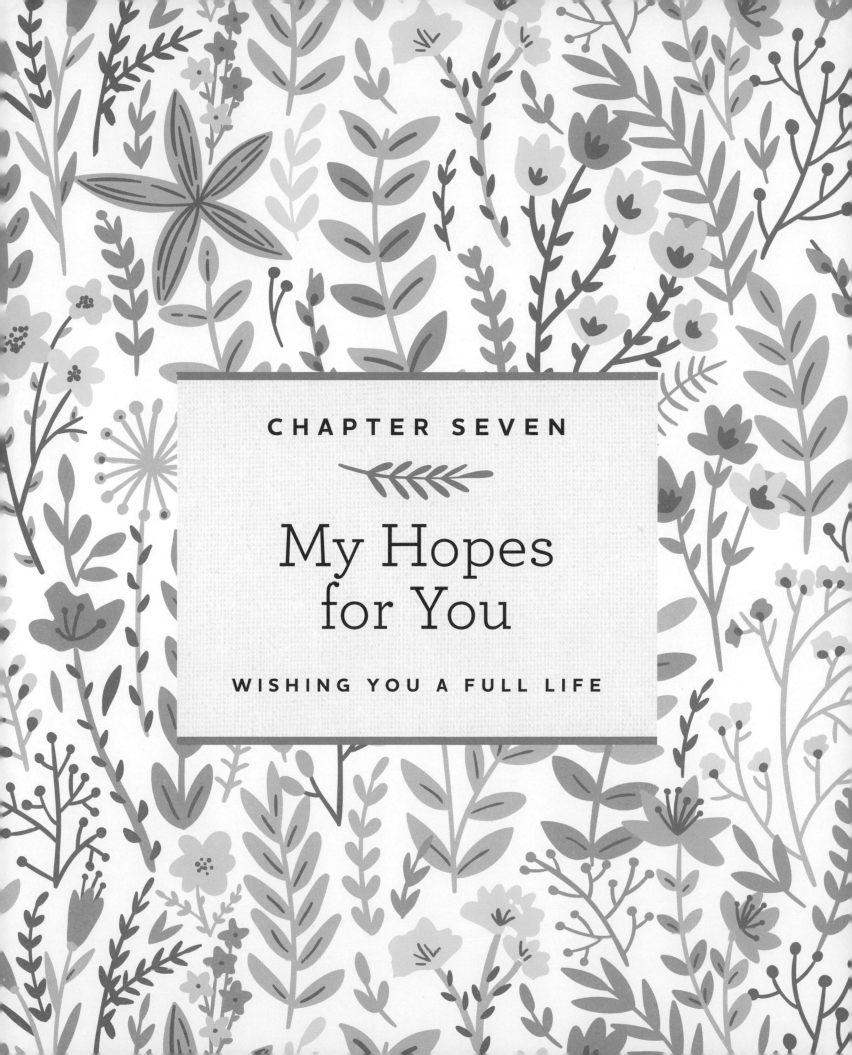

CHAPTER SEVEN

My Hopes
for You

WISHING YOU A FULL LIFE

Hello, You

Grandchildren are the hands by which we take hold of heaven.

—UNKNOWN

How we met for the first time _____

_____

_____

_____

_____

_____

You've found your place in the family as _____

_____

_____

_____

_____

_____

One thing I think you have learned from your family is

_____

_____

_____

_____

_____

What I hope you have learned from me is _____

_____

_____

_____

_____

_____

_____

_____

If I could make three wishes for you, they would be _____

_____

_____

_____

_____

_____

You Are Unique

In order to be irreplaceable,
one must always be different.

—COCO CHANEL

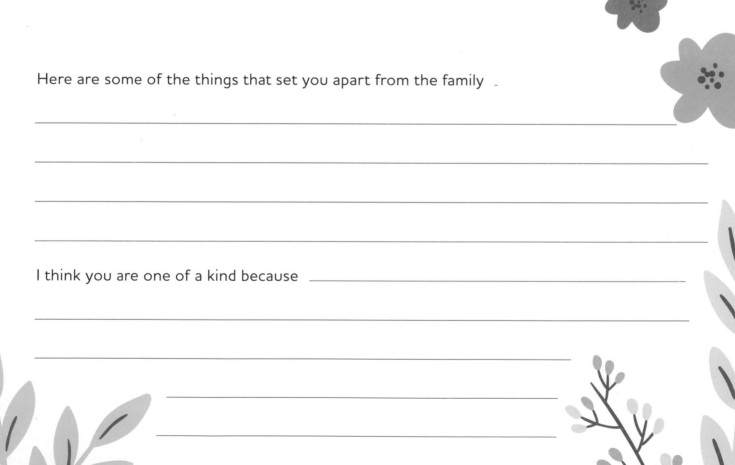

Here are some of the things that set you apart from the family

_____

_____

_____

_____

I think you are one of a kind because _____

_____

_____

_____

_____

You always make me laugh when you say _____

_____

_____

_____

_____

I love the way you show your unique self through _____

_____

_____

_____

_____

_____

My advice for staying the wonderful person you are is _____

_____

_____

_____

_____

_____

Sharing Dreams

You are never too old to set another goal or dream a new dream.

—C. S. LEWIS

My biggest hope for the future is _____

_____

_____

_____

I have so many dreams for you, including _____

_____

_____

_____

_____

_____

Some goals we can have together are _____

_____

_____

_____

_____

_____

You can realize your dreams by _____

_____

_____

_____

_____

_____

_____

_____

_____

I don't know everything, but these are some things I want you to know _____

_____

_____

_____

_____

_____

_____

Message to You

My story in this book is finished, but yours is just beginning. Here is a message from me to you, with all my love and wisdom.

_____

_____

_____

_____

_____

_____

_____

_____

_____

_____

_____

_____

_____

_____

_____